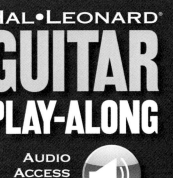

HAL•LEONARD®

GUITAR
PLAY-ALONG

AUDIO
ACCESS
INCLUDED

Early Rock
Instrumentals

PLAYBACK+
Speed • Pitch • Balance • Loop

To access audio visit:
www.halleonard.com/mylibrary

Enter Code
5795-7651-3046-3988

Tracking, mixing, and mastering by
Jim Reith at Beathouse Music
All Guitars by Doug Boduch
Bass by Tom McGirr
Keyboards by Warren Wiegratz
Drums by Scott Schroedl

ISBN 978-1-4234-5343-7

HAL•LEONARD®
7777 W. BLUEMOUND RD. P.O. BOX 13819 MILWAUKEE, WI 53213

Visit Hal Leonard Online at
www.halleonard.com

Guitar Notation Legend

THE MUSICAL STAFF shows pitches and rhythms and is divided by bar lines into measures. Pitches are named after the first seven letters of the alphabet.

TABLATURE graphically represents the guitar fingerboard. Each horizontal line represents a string, and each number represents a fret.

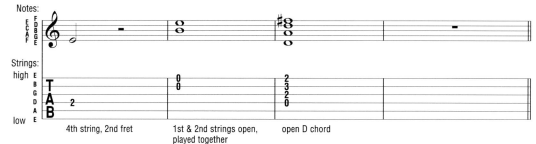

4th string, 2nd fret

1st & 2nd strings open, played together

open D chord

HALF-STEP BEND: Strike the note and bend up 1/2 step.

WHOLE-STEP BEND: Strike the note and bend up one step.

GRACE NOTE BEND: Strike the note and immediately bend up as indicated.

SLIGHT (MICROTONE) BEND: Strike the note and bend up 1/4 step.

BEND AND RELEASE: Strike the note and bend up as indicated, then release back to the original note. Only the first note is struck.

PRE-BEND: Bend the note as indicated, then strike it.

VIBRATO: The string is vibrated by rapidly bending and releasing the note with the fretting hand.

PALM MUTING: The note is partially muted by the pick hand lightly touching the string(s) just before the bridge.

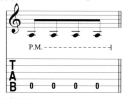

HAMMER-ON: Strike the first (lower) note with one finger, then sound the higher note (on the same string) with another finger by fretting it without picking.

PULL-OFF: Place both fingers on the notes to be sounded. Strike the first note and without picking, pull the finger off to sound the second (lower) note.

LEGATO SLIDE: Strike the first note and then slide the same fret-hand finger up or down to the second note. The second note is not struck.

SHIFT SLIDE: Same as legato slide, except the second note is struck.

TRILL: Very rapidly alternate between the notes indicated by continuously hammering on and pulling off.

TAPPING: Hammer ("tap") the fret indicated with the pick-hand index or middle finger and pull off to the note fretted by the fret hand.

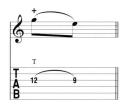

NATURAL HARMONIC: Strike the note while the fret-hand lightly touches the string directly over the fret indicated.

PINCH HARMONIC: The note is fretted normally and a harmonic is produced by adding the edge of the thumb or the tip of the index finger of the pick hand to the normal pick attack.

TREMOLO PICKING: The note is picked as rapidly and continuously as possible.

VIBRATO BAR DIVE AND RETURN: The pitch of the note or chord is dropped a specified number of steps (in rhythm), then returned to the original pitch.

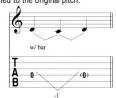

VIBRATO BAR SCOOP: Depress the bar just before striking the note, then quickly release the bar.

VIBRATO BAR DIP: Strike the note and then immediately drop a specified number of steps, then release back to the original pitch.

Additional Musical Definitions

(accent) • Accentuate note (play it louder).

(staccato) • Play the note short.

D.S. al Coda • Go back to the sign (%), then play until the measure marked "*To Coda*," then skip to the section labelled "**Coda**."

D.C. al Fine • Go back to the beginning of the song and play until the measure marked "*Fine*" (end).

Fill • Label used to identify a brief melodic figure which is to be inserted into the arrangement.

N.C. • Harmony is implied.

• Repeat measures between signs.

• When a repeated section has different endings, play the first ending only the first time and the second ending only the second time.

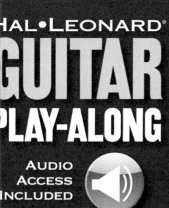

HAL•LEONARD®
GUITAR
PLAY-ALONG

AUDIO
ACCESS
INCLUDED

CONTENTS

Apache

By Jerry Lordan

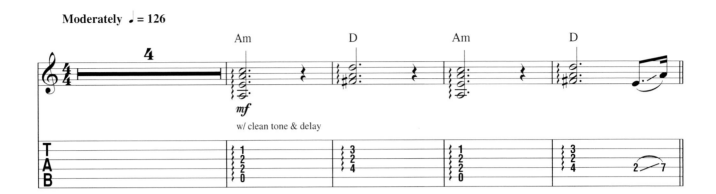

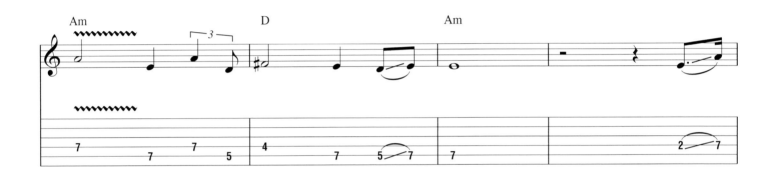

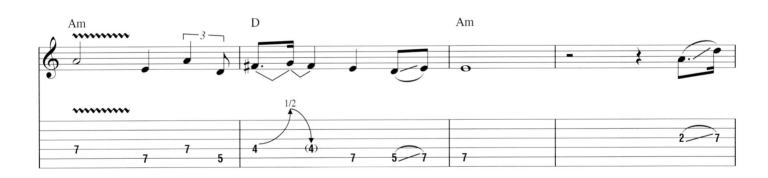

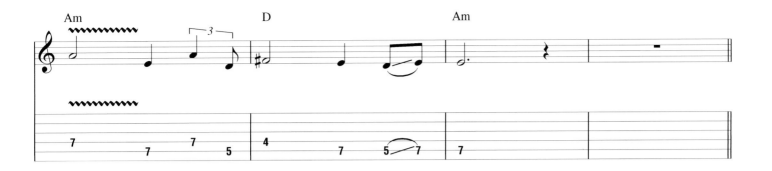

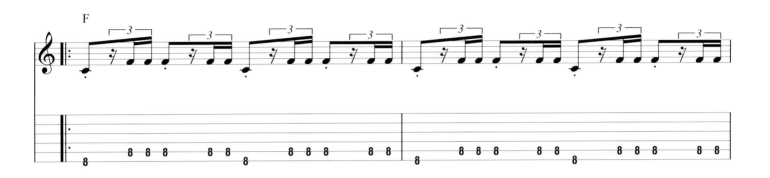

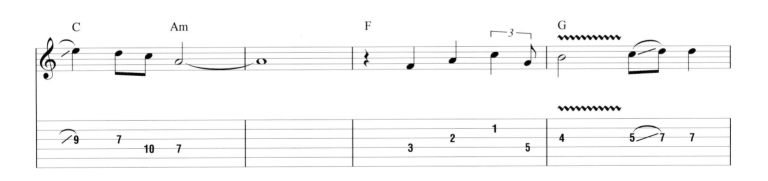

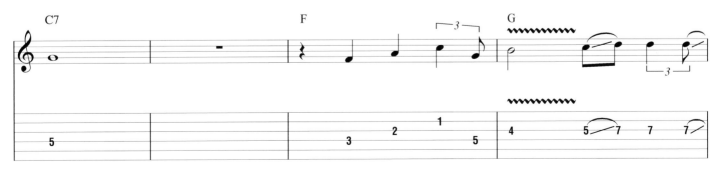

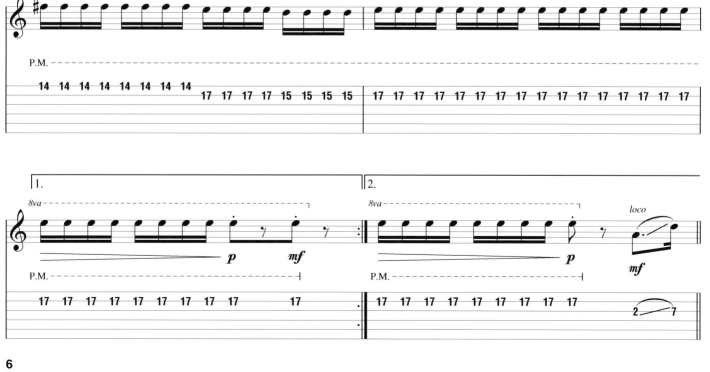

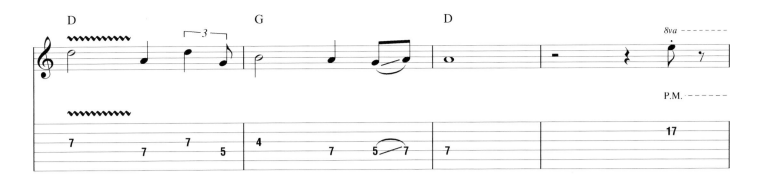

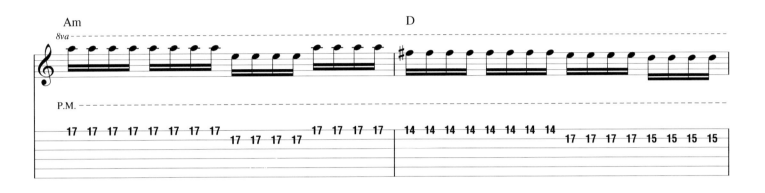

D.S. al Coda
(take repeat)

✦ Coda

Repeat and fade

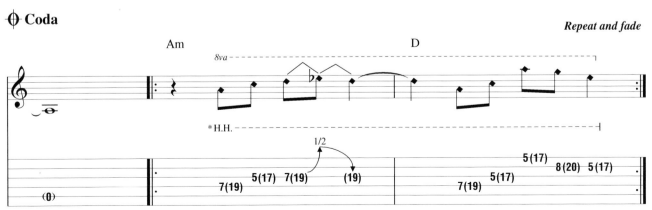

*While fretting the non-parenthetical tab number, lightly touch string w/ pick hand index finger at fret indicated in parentheses, then pluck the string from behind the index finger (towards bridge).

Guitar Boogie Shuffle

By Arthur Smith

Tune down 1/2 step:
(low to high) E♭-A♭-D♭-G♭-B♭-E♭

Moderately fast Shuffle ♩ = 180

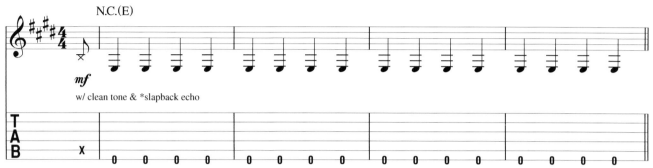

w/ clean tone & *slapback echo

*set for eighth-note triplet duration (110 ms) & 2 repeats

4th time, Fade out

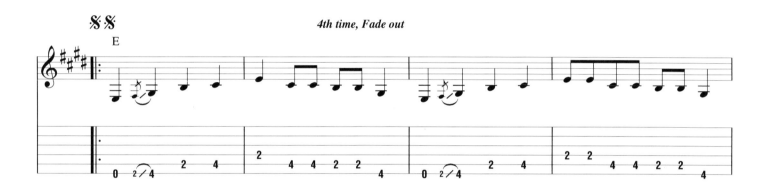

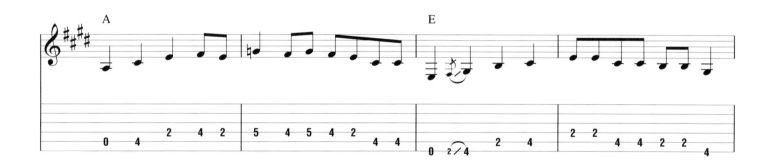

3rd time, Begin fade

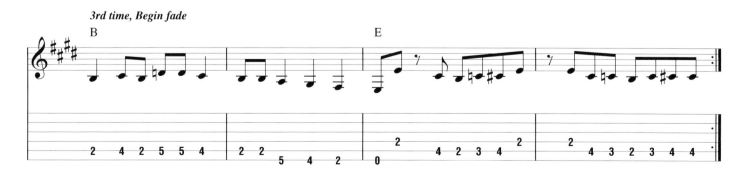

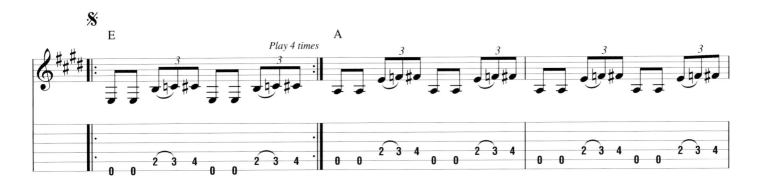

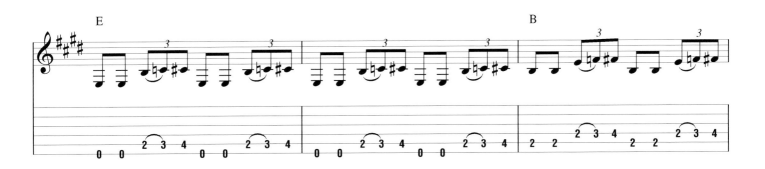

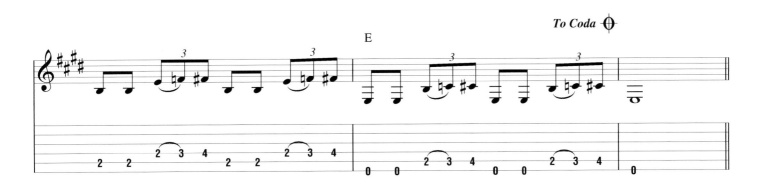

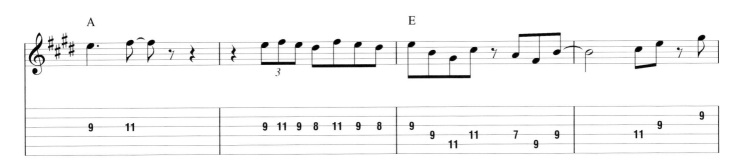

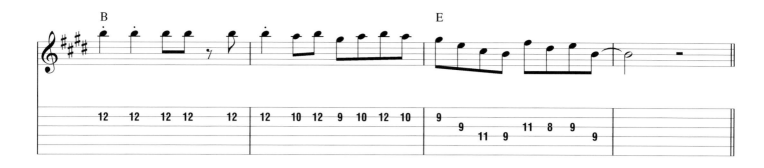

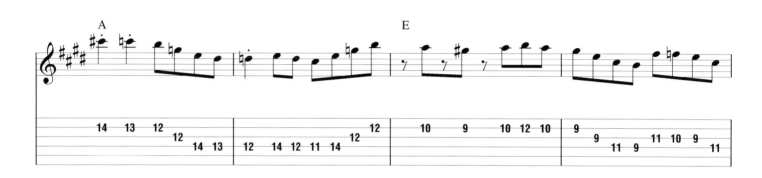

D.S. al Coda
(take repeats)

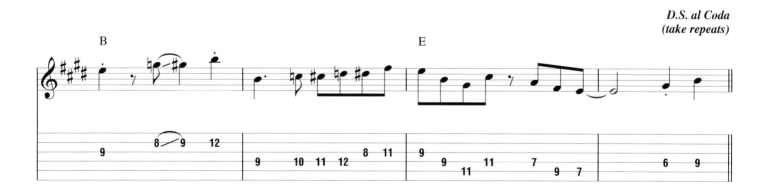

Coda

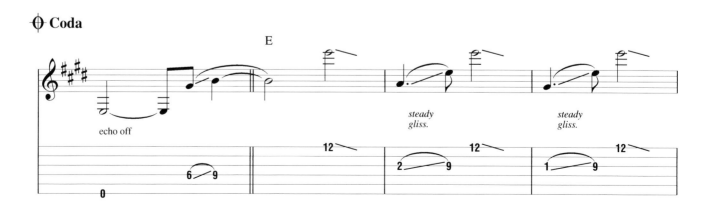

Raunchy

By William Justis and Sidney Manker

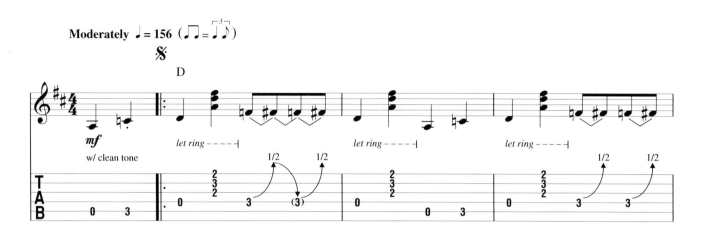

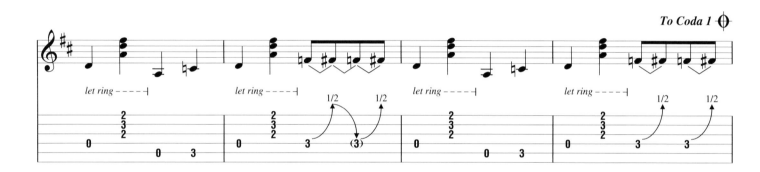

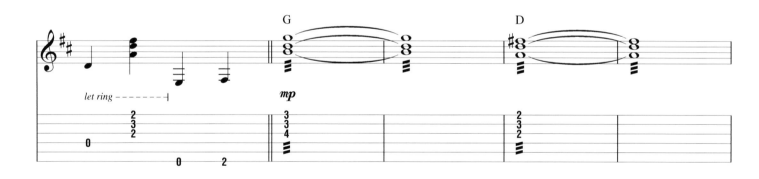

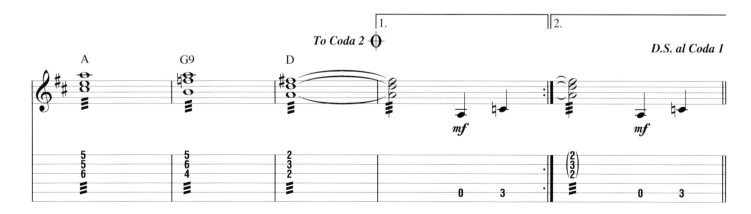

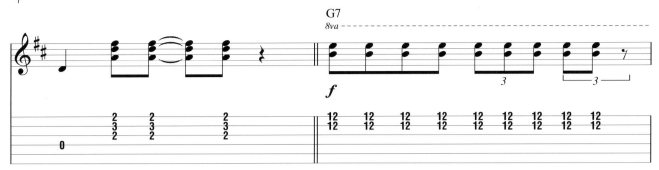

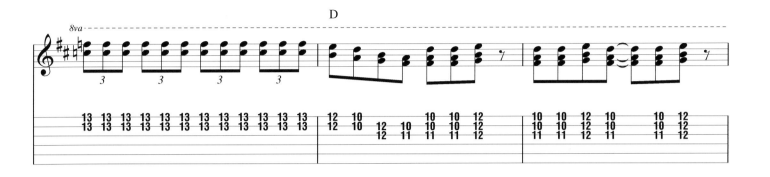

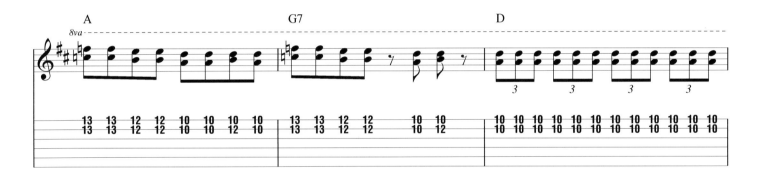

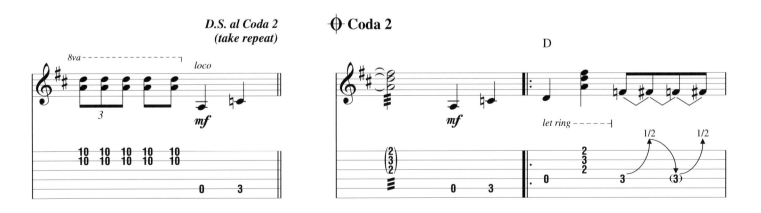

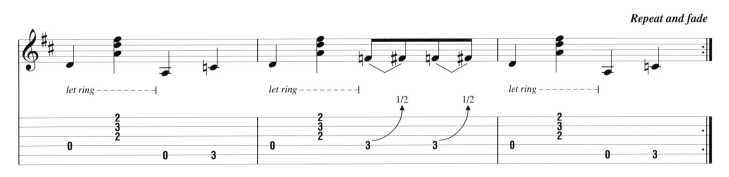

Rawhide

By Link Wray and Milt Grant

Bright Rock ♩ = 168

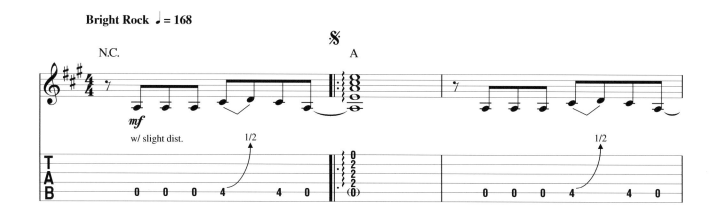

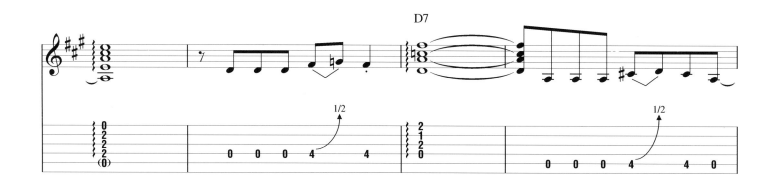

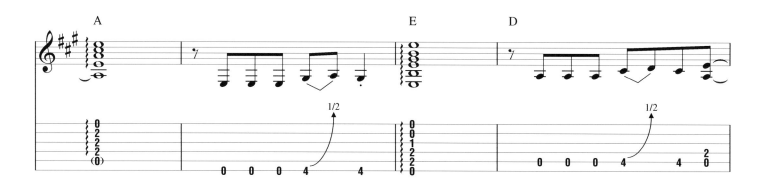

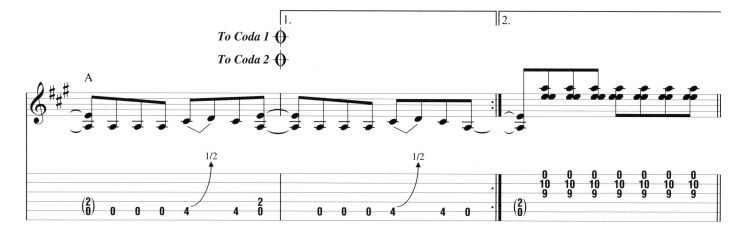

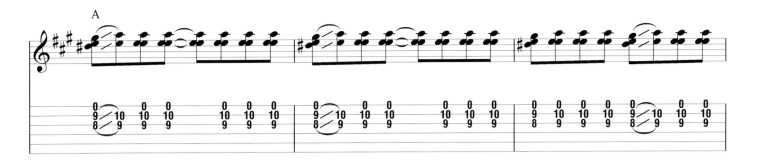

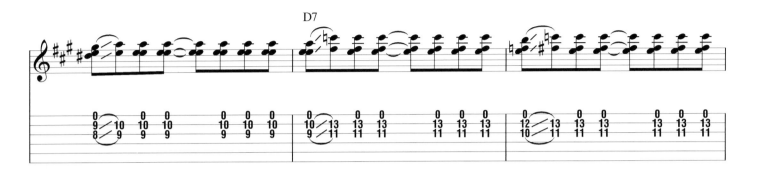

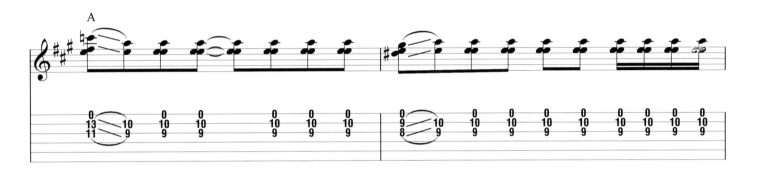

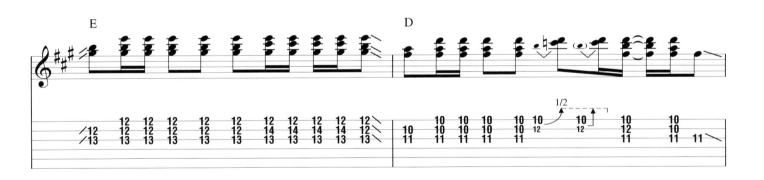

D.S. al Coda 1   ⊕ **Coda 1**

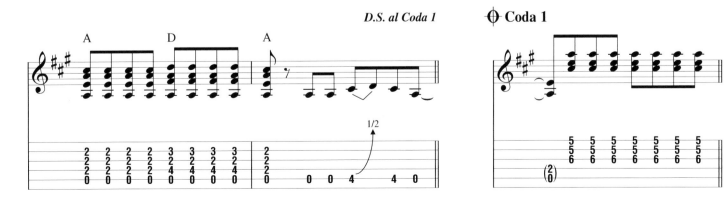

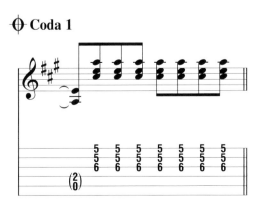

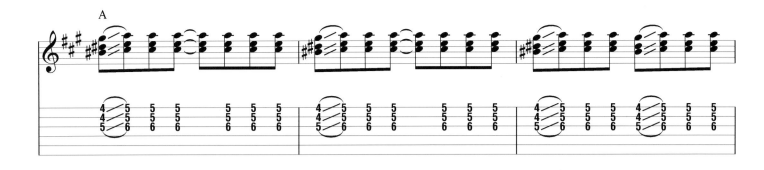

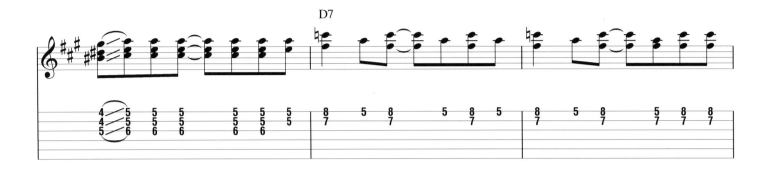

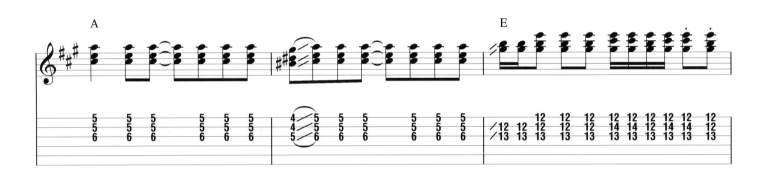

D.S. al Coda 2

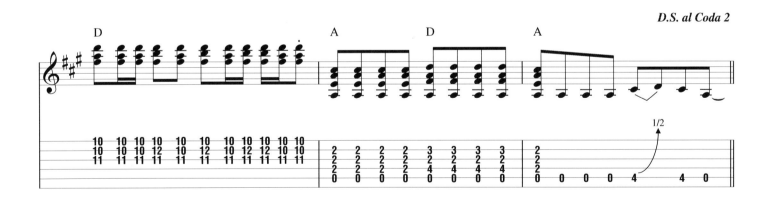

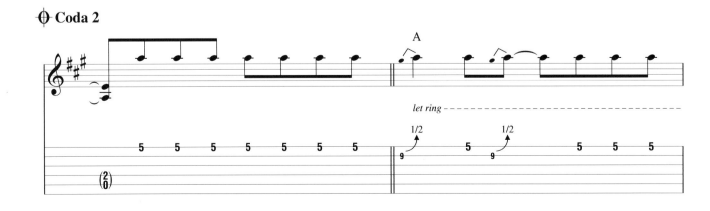

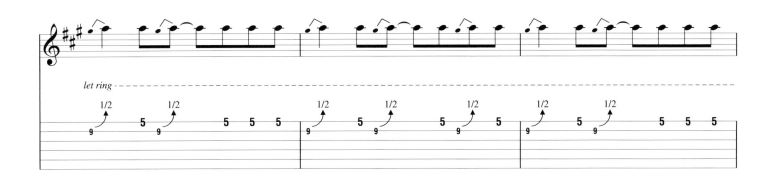

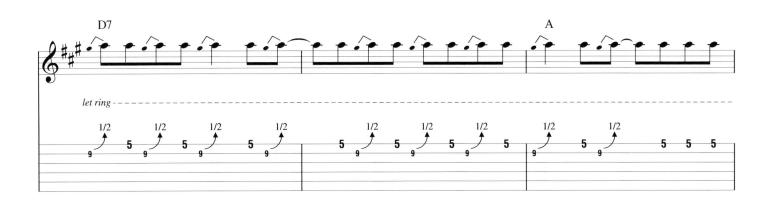

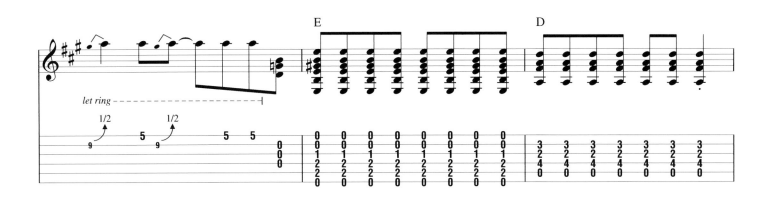

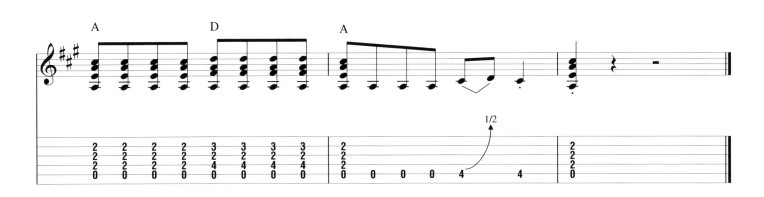

Rebel 'Rouser

By Duane Eddy and Lee Hazlewood

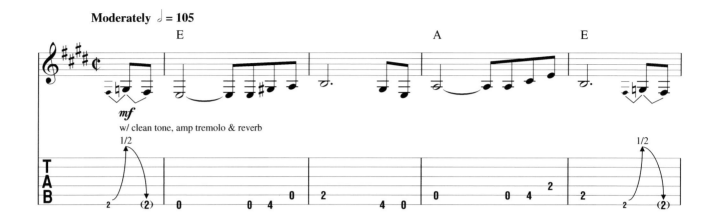

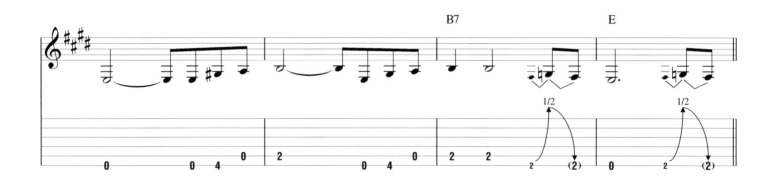

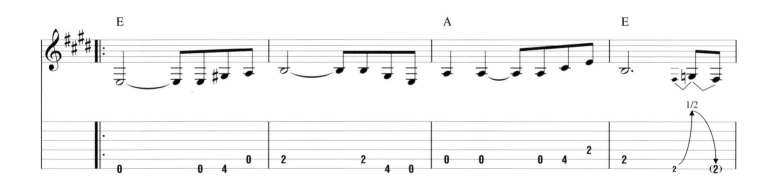

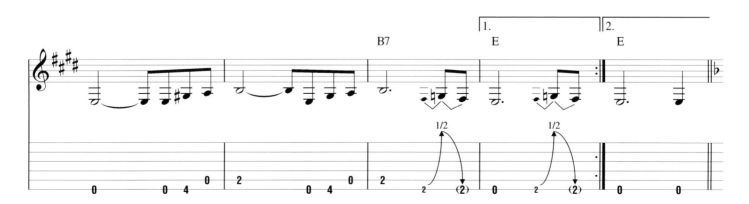

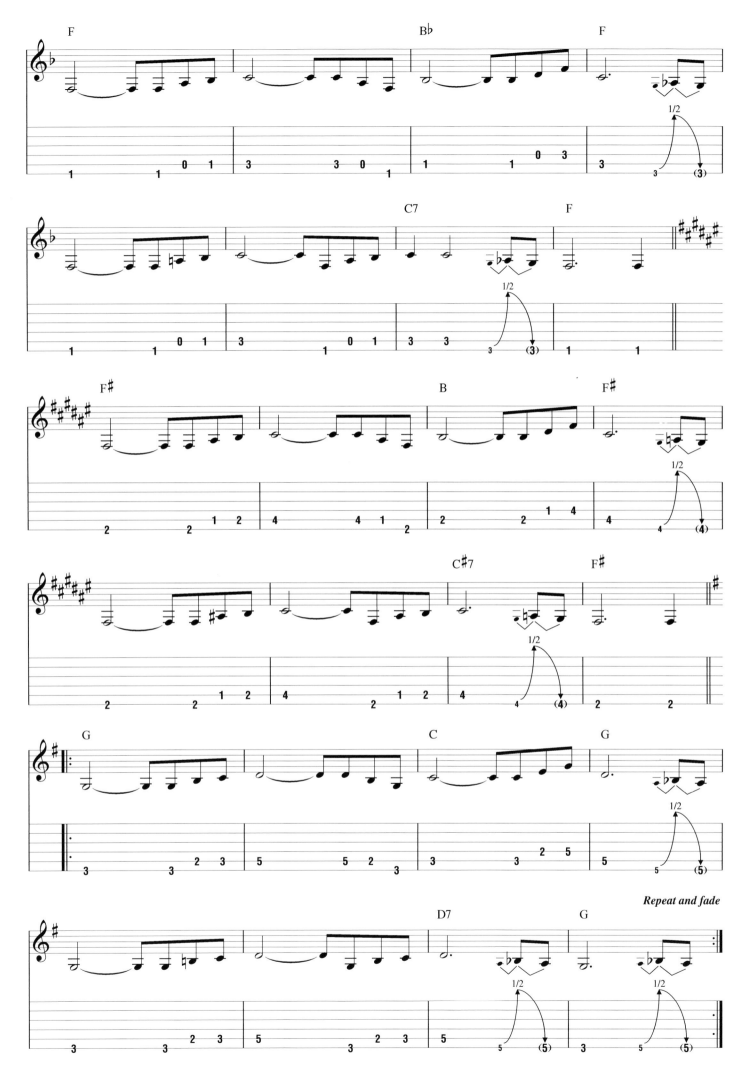

Repeat and fade

Sleepwalk

By Santo Farina, John Farina and Ann Farina

Open C6 tuning:
(low to high) G-C-E-G-A-C

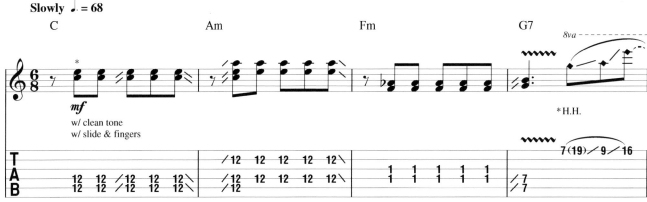

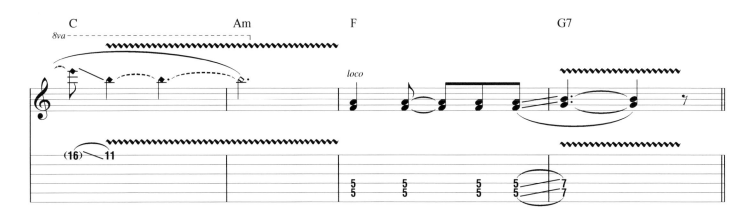

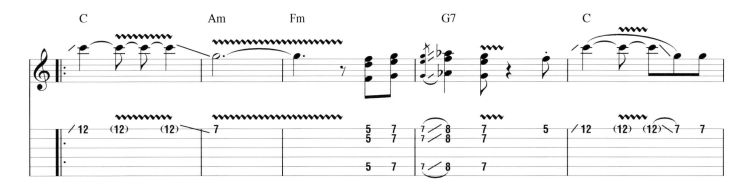

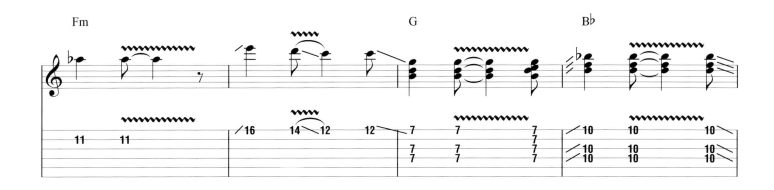

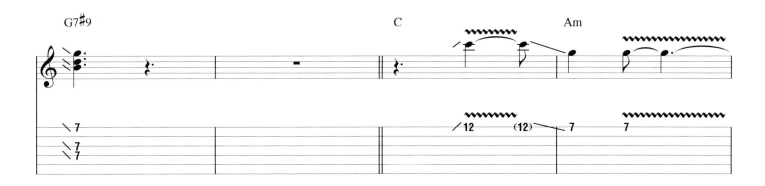

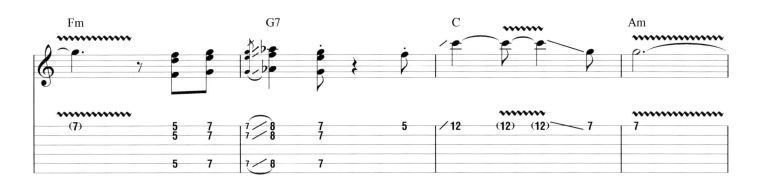

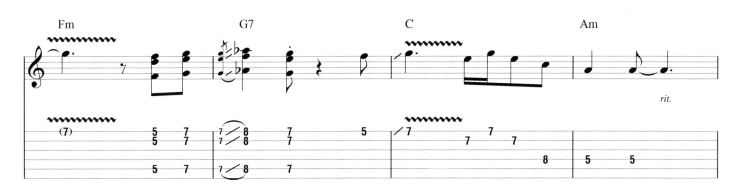

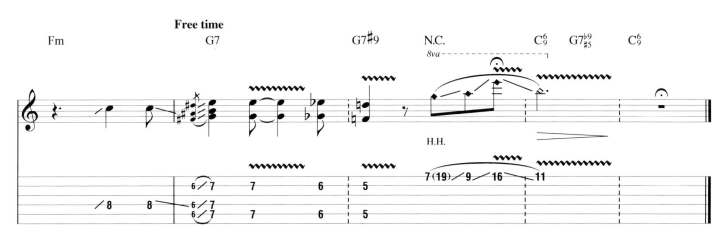

Telstar

By Joe Meek

Moderately fast ♩ = 144

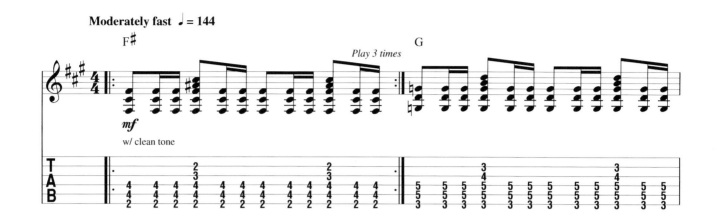

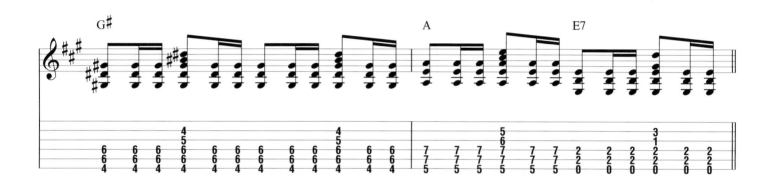

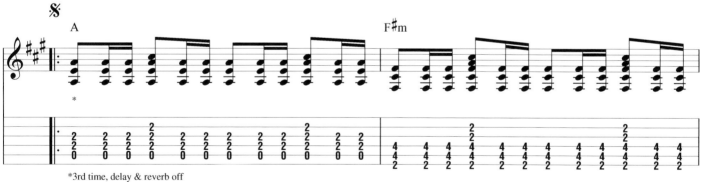

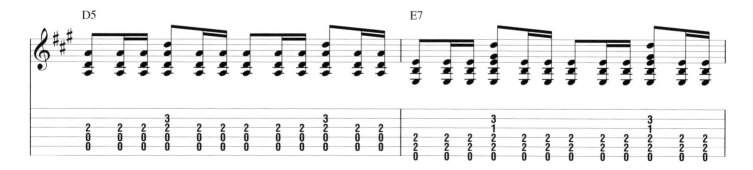

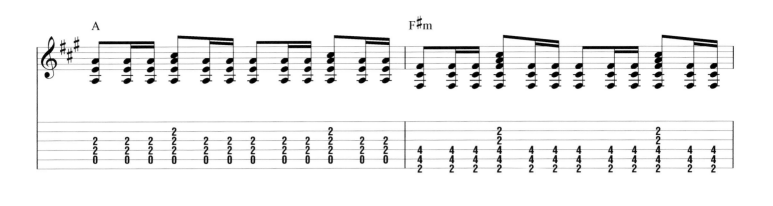

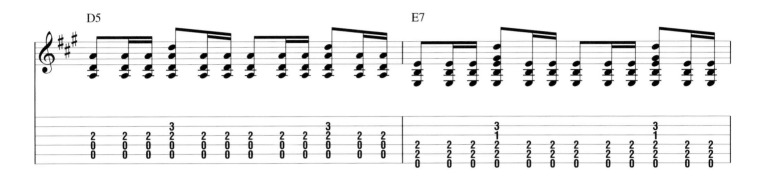

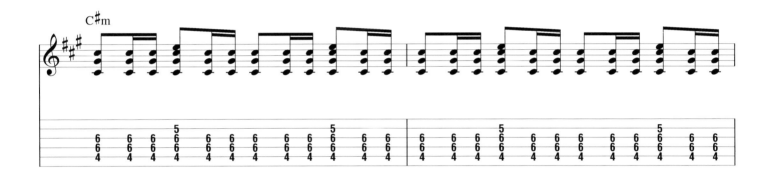

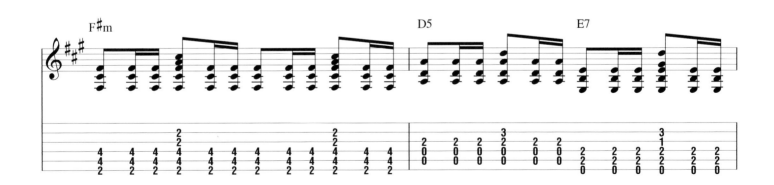

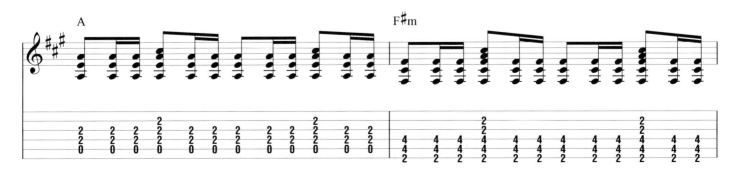

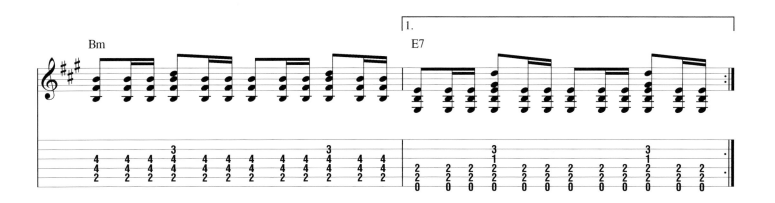

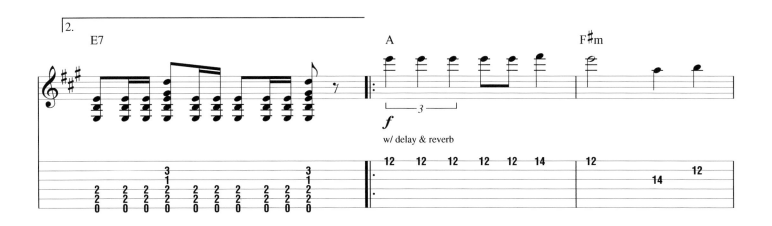

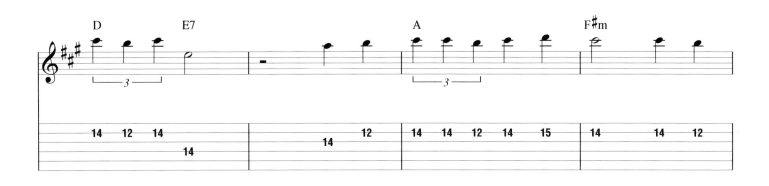

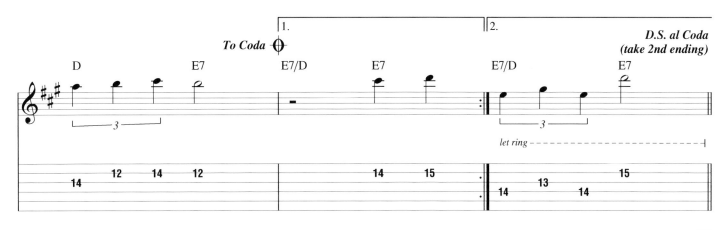

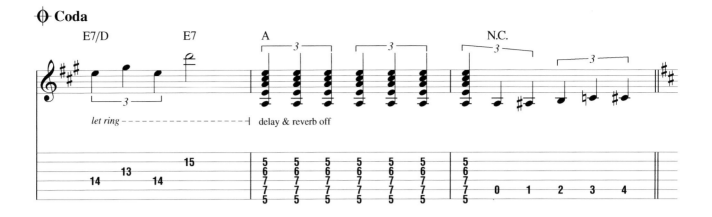

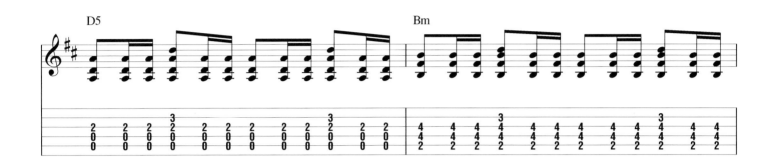

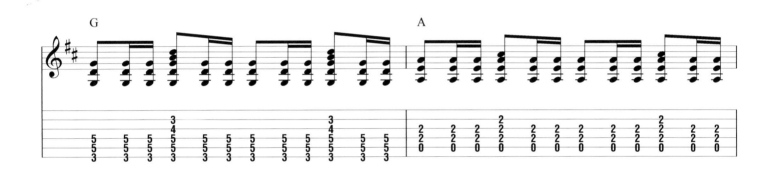

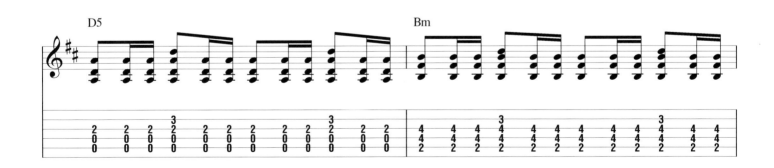

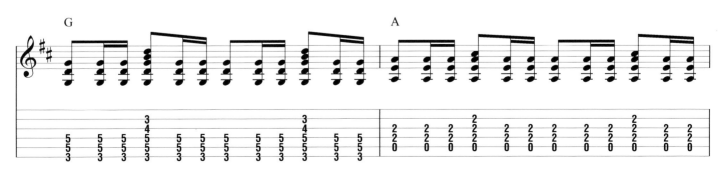

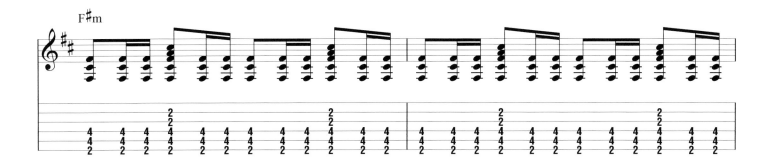

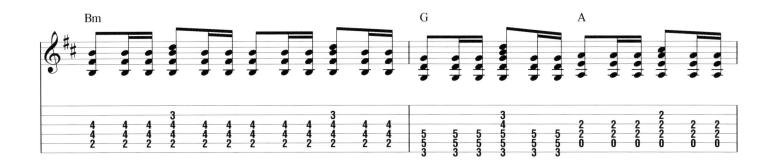

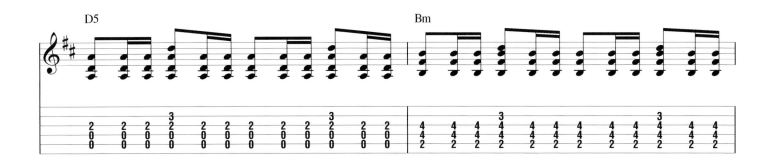

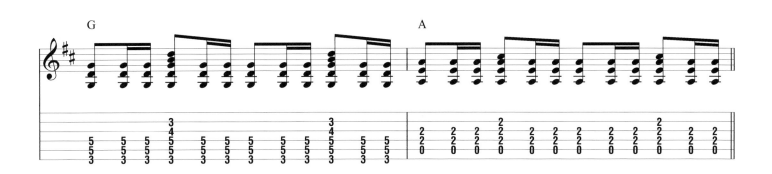

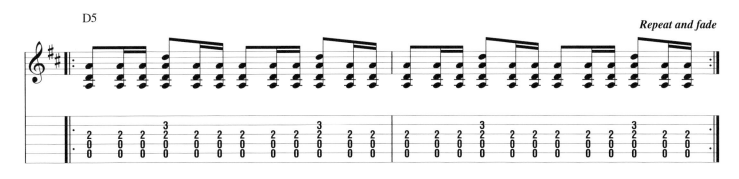

Tequila

By Chuck Rio

Moderately fast ♩ = 184

mf

w/ clean tone

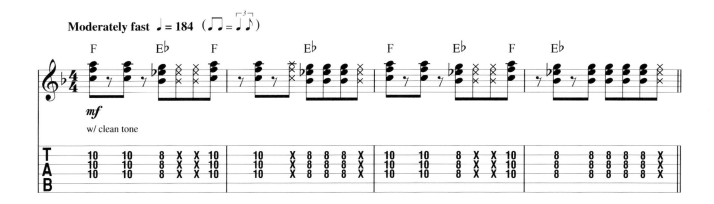

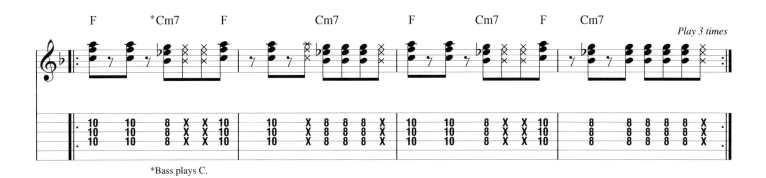

*Bass plays C.

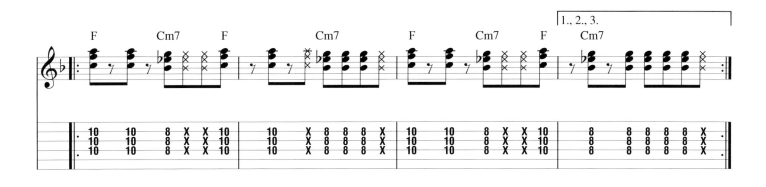

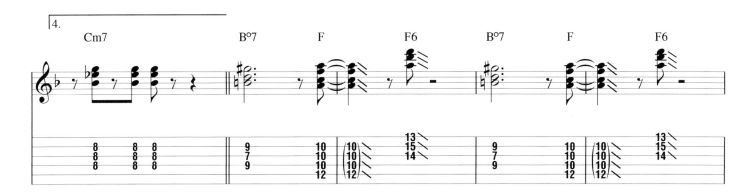

Spoken: Tequila.

Spoken: Tequila.

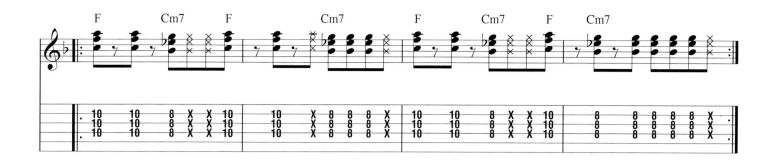

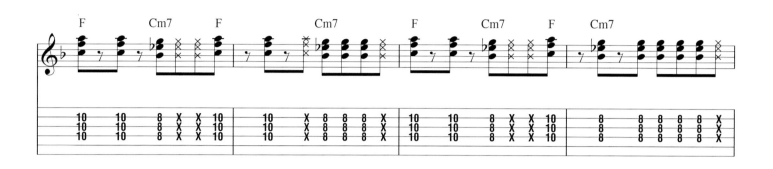

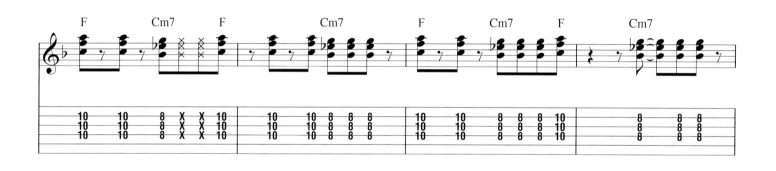

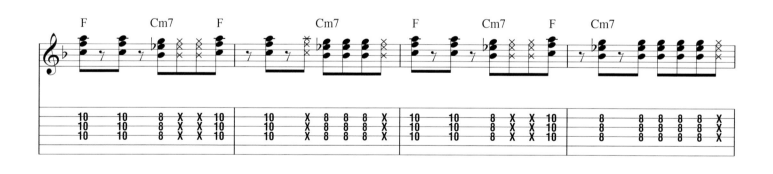

Shouted: Tequila!

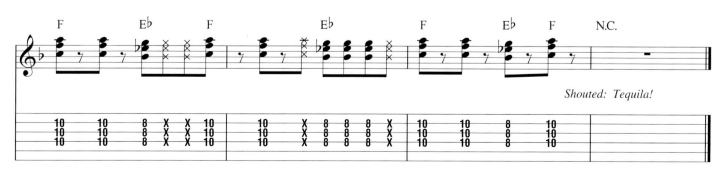